Read-It-All™ Books

An interactive high-interest/low-level reading series

Teacher's Manual

Readability Level: 3rd Grade
Interest Level: Grade 4 and Up

Ruth Nathan, Ph.D.
Series Consultant

LeapFrog SchoolHouse
Emeryville, CA 94608

Editorial, Design, and Production
by Bonnie Brook, Judy Nayer, and Thomasina Webb

Photo credits:
Cover:
© Paul Hardy/CORBIS (London Eye)
© DIDRIK JOHNCK/CORBIS SYGMA (Eric Weihenmeyer)
© David McNew/Getty Images (Forest Service Firefighter)

©2003 by LeapFrog Enterprises, Inc.

All rights reserved. No part of this publication may be reproduced or transmitted in any form or by any means, electronic or mechanical including photocopying, recording, or in a storage retrieval system, without permission in writing from LeapFrog Enterprises, Inc.

Permission is hereby granted to reproduce the Blackline Master pages bearing a copyright line, in limited quantities, for classroom use only.

LEAPFROG SCHOOLHOUSE, the LeapFrog SchoolHouse logo,
QUANTUM PAD, READ-IT-ALL, the Green GO Circle, and the Checker Border are trademarks of LeapFrog Enterprises, Inc. All other trademarks herein are the property of their respective owners.

ISBN: 1-59319-017-4
Printed in the U.S.A.
10 9 8 7 6 5 4 3 2 1   10 09 08 07 06 05 04 03

LeapFrog SchoolHouse, a division of LeapFrog Enterprises, Inc.
Emeryville, CA 94608
(800) 883-7430
www.LeapFrogSchoolHouse.com

Contents

Introduction and Philosophy	2
Word Analysis and Comprehension Skills	4
Using the Program	5
Getting Started	5
Features of Each *Read-It-All*™ Book	10

Lesson Plans
Book 1: *Amazing Inventions*	16
Book 2: *Outdoor Adventures*	20
Book 3: *Nature's Fury*	24

Blackline Masters
Class/Student Record Sheet	28
Articles I've Read	29
My Review	30
How to Use Read-It-All™ *Clues*	31
Now I Know!	32
Book 1: *Amazing Inventions*	33
Book 2: *Outdoor Adventures*	38
Book 3: *Nature's Fury*	43

Parent Letters (English and Spanish)
Book 1: *Amazing Inventions*	48
Book 2: *Outdoor Adventures*	50
Book 3: *Nature's Fury*	52
Answer Key ("Super Challenge!" Questions)	54

Read-It-All™ Books

Introduction and Philosophy

Welcome to the *Read-It-All™ Books* program, a series of nonfiction books designed for use with the unique Quantum Pad™ platform. The program targets struggling readers in the upper elementary grades. Each book in the series includes five engaging, easy-to-read articles organized around a high-interest theme. A number of articles have been adapted from a highly respected children's magazine, and others have been commissioned specifically for this program. Along with interactive multisensory experiences made possible through the Quantum Pad™ platform, and a host of activities recommended throughout this Teacher's Manual, these books allow a wide range of opportunities for successful reading and learning to occur.

What We Know About Helping Struggling Readers to Succeed

We know that to become proficient readers, students need to read, read, read. It sounds simple, but unfortunately, many children do not engage in much voluntary reading, and many less-skilled readers don't enjoy reading at all. All too often, struggling readers are given material that is too hard for them. When word recognition is slow and difficult, comprehension is often lost. When students don't understand what they are reading, the experience simply is not an enjoyable one—and there is no incentive to read. But students who avoid books can never engage in enough reading to become good readers. That's why it's critical to provide students with texts that are at just the right level for them—texts they can actually read.

We also know that students need to be motivated to read. The challenge is that for struggling readers, books at the right reading level are often way below their interest level and stage of cognitive development. Teachers say that it is especially hard to find nonfiction books that are interesting and engaging, as well as easy to read. Since students in the upper elementary grades are expected to read their content-area textbooks, it is essential to prepare students by giving them reading practice with nonfiction material that they can navigate.

The *Read-It-All™ Books* program is based on a simple formula aimed at reading success for the struggling reader:

Give students texts they *can* read
+
Give students texts they *want* to read
=
A successful reading experience
=
A positive attitude toward reading

Once students develop a positive attitude toward reading and gain access to appropriate texts, they'll want to read more and more. And when students begin to read more on their own, they are on their way to becoming fluent readers.

How Our Program Reflects the Needs of Struggling Readers

Matching students to texts We make it easy for you to match students to "just-right texts" by providing readability scores using the ATOS™ Readability Formula for Books, a system that works especially well for nonfiction texts. The ATOS™ formula analyzes the number of words per sentence, the average grade level of words, and the number of letters per word as indicators of text difficulty. The readability ranges for each book in *Read-It-All™ Books* adhere to the educational benchmark validated by research that materials should be at least two grade levels below a struggling reader's frustration level.

To match each student to the appropriate level of text difficulty, use the opening article in each *Read-It-All™* book as a screening device. Keep in mind, however, that with the support of the Quantum Pad™ platform, it is likely that students will want to explore materials that may appear difficult at first glance. Give them the opportunity! Once they've had a taste of success, they will want to take on new challenges.

Motivating students to read After selecting both enticing and interesting nonfiction material, we organized it around high-interest themes. To be sure we'd attract students' interest, we added vivid photographs and illustrations that support the text, as well as a magazine-style design. The engaging, interactive technology of the Quantum Pad™ platform combined with high-interest content adds up to a whole lot of fun in the context of a highly motivating reading experience.

Helping students to read independently The technology integrated into the Quantum Pad™ platform helps students successfully read books that they might not otherwise be able to read. By providing audio assistance and immediate feedback, the Quantum Pad™ platform provides instructional reading support similar to what a teacher might provide in a one-on-one or small-group guided reading session. Yet, by making the independent reading experience possible, students get an extra boost of self-esteem that has a great impact on their attitude toward reading. Students become motivated to practice reading on their own, begin to read independently for learning and enjoyment, and achieve greater fluency and proficiency—which leads to greater comprehension!

Teaching reading strategies By removing the roadblocks to fluency, we are able to provide reading instruction appropriate to the grade level. We can also provide strategies that will help students build vocabulary and increase comprehension, including higher-level thinking skills. The Quantum Pad™ technology delivers in a dialogue format skill lessons that provide students with explicit demonstrations of the strategies good readers use when they read. By embedding these strategies right in the text, we are helping to ensure that students learn how to become active readers. Through modeling, we hope to build the habits of good readers.

Word Analysis Skills

BREAK IT DOWN

Syllabication

Prefixes

Compound Words

Suffixes/Inflectional Endings

Derivations

Comprehension Skills

WORD CLUE *(Context Clues)*

THE BIG IDEA *(Main Idea)*

FIND THE DETAILS *(Details)*

WHY DID IT HAPPEN? *(Cause and Effect)*

WHAT'S NEXT? *(Predict Outcomes)*

WHAT DO YOU THINK? *(Draw Conclusions)*

SUM IT UP *(Summarize)*

FACT OR OPINION? *(Fact and Opinion)*

FIGURE IT OUT *(Make Inferences)*

SAME OR DIFFERENT ? *(Compare and Contrast)*

WHAT'S THE ORDER? *(Sequence)*

Using the Program

The Quantum Pad™ Platform Technology

The Quantum Pad™ platform is a classroom learning system that allows books to talk. Using a stylus, or special pen, students can hear words read aloud, listen to the definitions of unfamiliar words, obtain information from pictures and captions, and access reading tips. Volume controls can be monitored by touching [+] and [-]. Because of the audio assistance and immediate feedback provided with the Quantum Pad™ platform, virtually any student can enjoy a successful reading experience.

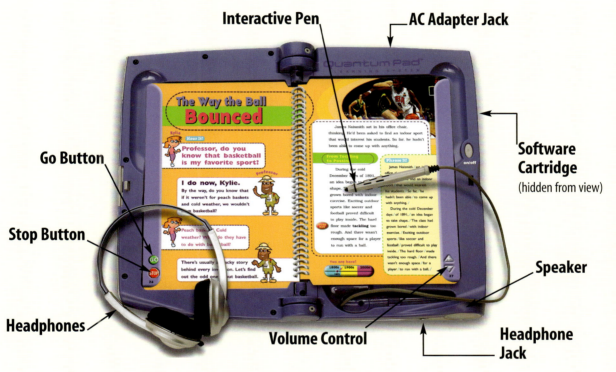

Getting Started

- Show students how to place the book on the Quantum Pad™ platform, turn on the power, and use the Quantum Pad™ pen to touch words, pictures, and icons. As students read, have them touch the green GO circle to activate the pages and the red STOP sign to stop what they are doing.

- Together, read aloud the introductory dialogue and the first page of one article to get students started. Invite volunteers to reread the dialogue to the class, acting out the parts of the student and the "know-it-all" professor. The "Hear It!" feature provides motivation and builds background for reluctant readers by allowing them to have the entire dialogue read to them.

- Point out the "Phrase It!" feature. Tell students that this feature shows them how good readers read in phrases rather than word by word. Have students first listen to the "Phrase It!" audio, then listen again and read along with it. Conclude by asking them to read the unmarked text on their own, incorporating the proper phrasing and expression.

- Show students how to touch a boldfaced word once to hear it pronounced and twice to hear its definition. Finally, use the procedure outlined on page 31 of this manual to show students how to access strategy tips through the icons in the margins. Later, give students the handout on page 32 to check what they've learned from the tips.

Interactive Reading Strategies That Offer Support

Each *Read-It-All*™ book provides specific strategies to build vocabulary, comprehension skills, and word analysis skills. Students can

- touch a boldfaced word once to hear it pronounced and twice to hear the definition;
- touch 🔵 to hear a student and a "know-it-all" professor hammering out a word-attack strategy; and
- touch 🔵, for example, and hear the same student and professor brainstorming ways to comprehend text—in this case, by identifying the main idea.

The learning becomes twofold: Students learn new information from the text while learning the strategies needed to read with greater understanding. (For the complete list of word analysis and comprehension skills, see page 4 of this manual.)

Ways to Monitor and Enrich Student Understanding

Each article is followed by a "Super Challenge" to check students' understanding. As they work through six multiple-choice questions, students earn points and receive one of three prizes, depending on the total number of points gained. Sound effects reward right answers, while gentle hints address incorrect responses and lead students toward the correct ones. A suggestion to review the article is provided to students who get zero points. "Fun Facts"—a bank of believe-it-or-not-type questions and answers—provides fascinating and sometimes amusing facts related to the book's theme. At the back of each book, "Super Challenge Championships," a glossary game, checks students' knowledge of structural and word analysis skills, as well as the meaning of boldfaced vocabulary words. On the inside back cover, "Know It All" activities provide theme-related opportunities to work independently or with others to read, write, listen, speak, and do research.

Flexible Teaching Options

The *Read-It-All*™ *Books* program is easily adapted for use in a variety of contexts, including in mainstream classrooms with struggling readers and English-language learners, in pull-out tutorial programs, in media centers, and even at home. The *Read-It-All*™ *Books* program can be used in your classroom in the following ways:

- ***Whole-class instruction*** can be planned around a theme, using the lesson plans in this manual. Each lesson contains theme-related instruction and activities of varying levels of difficulty, ensuring appropriate instruction for all students.
- ***Small-group activities*** that follow the reading can be conducted with children who are at the same proficiency level or at different levels. Practice in cooperative learning is greatly facilitated by placing students in small groups. The intimacy of the group helps promote participation of all group members in lively discussion and active exploration of the themes through reading, research, and writing. Themes can be integrated into reading assignments for reading groups. Then, as a group, students can complete the activities on the inside back covers.
- ***Individual tutoring*** can be used by teachers, aides, or parent volunteers to provide practice in vocabulary and comprehension skills. Individual instruction can also encourage oral language production with reluctant speakers. For example,

students who wish to practice their phrasing may feel more comfortable reading aloud in a one-on-one situation.

- *Independent reading* is easily facilitated once a book is placed on a Quantum Pad™ platform. The functionality allows students to be guided through the text; access skills support, as necessary; and obtain immediate feedback on his or her understanding of the article. The Quantum Pad™ platform can be used in school media centers, as well as in classroom learning centers, for independent work. Using the Quantum Pad™ platform with headphones, students can enjoy reading the books at their own pace.
- *Home* is the perfect place to help foster learning at school. Consider setting up a week-by-week schedule that allows for each student to take home a Quantum Pad™ platform and a book on Monday, to be returned on the following Monday. Suggest that the student and at least one other family member or caregiver read one of the articles together each day. On pages 48–53 of this Teacher's Manual, we have provided Parent Letters (in English and Spanish) that can be copied and sent home with the student.

Organization and Pacing

- The themes in the *Read-It-All™ Books* program can be used in any order. Each book includes practice in the key vocabulary and comprehension skills students need for reading success.
- The articles in each book all have readability levels within one grade level. Yet some articles are more challenging than others. To obtain the specific ATOS™ readability score for each article, refer to the chart on the first page of each lesson in this manual.
- Pacing is flexible and can be adapted to your needs and your students' needs. For example, you can spend five weeks on one theme—one week for each of the five articles in the book—or you can accelerate coverage of a theme into a week or two.
- The program also offers the option of allowing teachers to present articles as stand-alone selections rather than selections tied to a specific theme. In this instance, students may be assigned to work on individual articles from a book. Because they are short, the articles may be completed in a single session.

Assessment and Tracking Students' Progress

The Teacher's Manual includes a record-keeping sheet for tracking students' work. Teachers may record which articles and activities have been completed by each student, and when. Teachers may also jot down notes about students' performance and progress as they move from article to article and book to book.

At the end of each lesson, a list of Assessment Tips offers teachers some strategies for monitoring students' skill development in comprehension and reading fluency, vocabulary and word analysis, and writing for a variety of purposes. Additionally, suggestions are provided for assessing oral language development.

Amazing Inventions *in this book*

Articles	ATOS Readability	Word Analysis Skills	Comprehension Skills	Vocabulary
Crunch! The Pretzel Story	3.6	Suffix: -y	Sequence Compare and Contrast Context Clues	automated, folktale, instantly, loopy, monks, religious, moist, popular, tradition, yeast
Chester Greenwood's Ears	3.5	Prefix: in- Suffix/Inflectional Ending: -ed	Details Main Idea Context Clues	allergic, flannel, frostbitten, granted, hinges, invention, necessity, patent, sport, velvet
Wheels in His Head	3.5	Suffix: -tion	Draw Conclusions Fact and Opinion Context Clues	collapse, daring, experienced, foundation, grand, observation, officials, passengers, platform, wonder
The Way the Ball Bounced	3.7	Syllabication	Make Inferences Summarize Context Clues	arc, balcony, dribble, grooves, injuries, inventiveness, passing, physical education, steal, tackling
The Mask That Saved Lives	3.6	Compound Words (1 word)	Cause and Effect Predict Outcomes Context Clues	breathing systems, disaster, explosion, factory, harbor, patented, staggered, tailor, unconscious, versions

Articles adapted from Highlights® for Children

about this book
THEME: Unusual inventions

Cold ears? Bored students? For inventors, a problem is just an invention waiting to happen! The results may seem unusual, but inventors add fun and flavor to our lives, and sometimes save them! Each invention in this book has a story behind it.

- "**Crunch! The Pretzel Story**" reveals the secret history of this tasty snack. The article travels back in time to find the pretzel's origin in the monasteries of southern Europe, then moves forward to explore its use and form over the centuries.
- "**Chester Greenwood's Ears**" were the problem. They always got cold when Chester went outside to brave Maine's frosty winter weather. But when Chester combined wire, fur, and flannel to create an amazing accessory, his problem was solved, and the earmuff was born.
- In 1893, officials for the Chicago World's Fair were shocked when a young inventor first described his idea for a massive observation wheel. "**Wheels in His Head**" describes how George Ferris took an idea from his imagination and brought the Ferris wheel to life.
- When a young gym teacher needed a new indoor game to keep his students active during winter, he came up with basketball. "**The Way the Ball Bounced**" explains how one man's inspiration forever changed the world of sports.
- While it may have looked strange, there was nothing silly about Garrett Morgan's invention of the gas mask. His "Safety Hood" became "**The Mask That Saved Lives**" when he demonstrated its worth to firefighters in a daring tunnel rescue. Today, rescue workers and soldiers are forever grateful for Morgan's invention.

Whether tasty, entertaining, or essential, each of these inventions plays a part in our lives. Encourage students to find out the untold story behind each amazing invention.

Write About It!
Hello World
Ask students to imagine that each invention described in the book (*pretzel, gas mask, earmuffs, basketball, Ferris wheel*) is a brand-new invention. Then, invite them to make a poster to announce one of these inventions to the public. Have students brainstorm what information they will include in their posters. Tell them to ask themselves, *Who will buy the invention? Why will people want it?* Encourage students to write creative copy—using prose or poetry—and to use descriptive words, too. Remind students that a good poster needs a strong picture and just a few words. Have students first plan the poster on a small sheet of paper, encouraging them to use all the space, before drawing on a larger sheet. Hang posters on classroom walls.

Time Capsule
Explain to students that time capsules are containers that are filled with present-day objects. The capsules are then buried to help people in the future understand life in the past. Invite students to work in groups to choose five modern inventions that they would include in a time capsule for today. Point out that each invention should provide important insight into the way we live today for the people who uncover the capsule. Students should write a few sentences about each invention to include with the capsule. To help students get started, copy and distribute the **Write About It!** blackline master on page 35 of this manual.

You Are There!
Ask students to imagine they are news reporters, experiencing one of the inventions from the book for the very first time, e.g., they are taking the first ride on a Ferris wheel; they are in the crowd, watching the first game of basketball; they are on site at a tunnel disaster and see Morgan's Safety Hood for the first time. Have students write an on-the-scene report, describing the event and the invention. Remind students to include the 5Ws of good reporting—*who, what, where, when,* and *why*—in their articles. Encourage volunteers to read their articles to the class. Record student work in a "nightly news broadcast" show on audio or video.

Do a Project!
Invention Convention
Tell students that during the next month they will work in groups to create exhibits for an Invention Convention. Explain that a convention is a large gathering of people with common interests. Have each group select an invention as the subject of its exhibit—an invention that the group believes is "the most important ever."

To get started, copy and distribute the **Do a Project!** blackline master on page 36 of this manual. Review with students the process of creating an exhibit.

Brainstorm and Select Explain to students that at this stage, they should work together in a group to choose an invention that they believe has been critically important in history. The invention can date as far back as the wheel or it may be as recent as the MP3 player. Encourage each student to make suggestions; then have the group select one.

Research Explain to students that they should now gather information about the invention: its inventor or inventors, the era in which it was created, its changes and improvements over the years, and its benefits to the world.

Plan Using their research, students should begin planning what their exhibit will look like and what they wish to include. Invite students to consider multimedia possibilities, including photographs, audio, video, slideshows, or interactive computer programs. Groups should assign roles to each member to create visual aids, as well as written or recorded text.

Assemble and Examine Students should work together to complete and then review each aspect of their work. Encourage students to invite a few observers to preview their exhibit.

Display and Discuss Have groups take turns presenting their exhibits to classmates. Afterward, initiate a class discussion about what students learned from creating their own exhibits and from viewing the exhibits of others.

Teacher Support
The Teacher's Manual

The Teacher's Manual provides three lessons—one for each theme—that include

- *an overview for each book,* including ATOS™ readability scores, skills, and vocabulary for each article;
- *an introduction to each theme,* including a summary of each article and how the article fits into the theme;
- *tips and strategies for using the student books,* including prereading strategies and activities that integrate the theme with reading and language arts;
- *multilevel activities,* including writing ideas ranging from writing captions for photographs to writing a play; content-area activities that link each theme to science, social studies, geography, mathematics, and the arts; and long-term projects that call upon students to "go beyond the book" and research one aspect of the theme for an extended period of time;
- *suggestions for ELL (English Language Learners),* including specific activities that build vocabulary and comprehension skills;

- ***reproducible student activity pages (blackline masters),*** including activities for word work, comprehension, writing, map skills development, and research. Each lesson offers five theme-related activity pages. In addition, each Teacher's Manual includes four blackline masters for use with any lesson: **1)** *Class/Student Record Sheet*—a record-keeping form for teachers to track students' progress; **2)** *Articles I've Read*—a reading log where students can keep track of the articles they've read; **3)** *My Review*—a book review form for students to complete; and **4)** *Now I Know!*—a handout for students to process what they have learned from reading strategy tips;

- ***assessment tips,*** including ideas for portfolio assessment and assessment of student performance individually, with small groups, and as part of the whole class;

- ***a bibliography*** of fiction, nonfiction, and poetry, as well as Web sites that tie in to the theme and allow opportunities for further research and investigation;

- ***parent letters*** to maintain the home/school connection. These letters, in English and Spanish, explain what children are reading and offer activities to do at home.

9

Features of Each Read-It-All™ Book

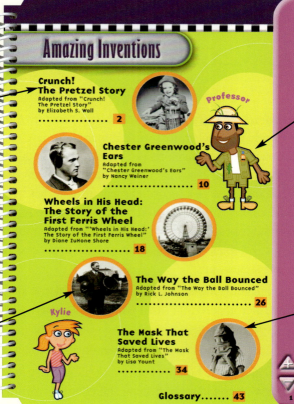

Each book includes 5 easy-to-read, nonfiction articles linked by a high-interest, content-area theme.

When students touch any title or photograph, they hear a summary of the article. This preview motivates readers and helps them choose what they want to read.

Each article is read by a "know-it-all" professor, in this case a scientist, who interacts with a curious student.

Exciting interactive photographs—just like in a magazine—add interest and support the text.

Research shows...

Two major stumbling blocks get in the way of success for students during content reading: uninteresting texts and too many difficult words. High-interest, easily accessible texts support readers' success.

- See Fry, E. (2002). Readability versus leveling. *The Reading Teacher, 56 (3),* 286–291.
- National Center for Education Statistics (1994). NAEP 1992 trends in academic progress. Washington, D.C.: U.S. Department of Education.

The page layout and design mimic a magazine.

Readers can hurdle barriers in decoding by touching any unknown word to hear it spoken aloud.*

New and difficult words are presented as vocabulary words in bold type. Readers can touch boldfaced words once to hear them pronounced and twice to hear the definitions. This feature helps build students' knowledge of content-area vocabulary.

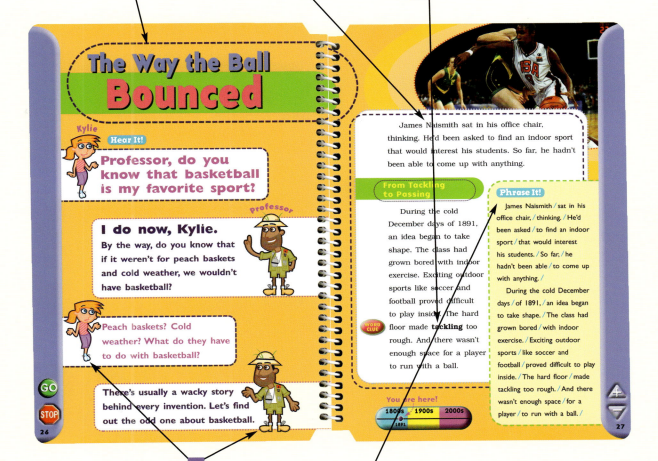

An introductory conversation activates prior knowledge and creates interest in each article by offering intriguing clues about its subject.

The Phrase It! feature models the reading of text in phrases, a strategy that builds reading fluency. Readers see and hear how to read in phrases rather than word by word.

Research shows...

Just as fluent and proficient readers organize text into phrases, or meaningful chunks, helping struggling readers to phrase text improves fluency and comprehension in reading.

- See Rasinski, T. V. (1994). Developing syntactic sensitivity in reading through phrase-cued texts. In B. Honig et al. (Eds.), *Reading research anthology: The why? of reading instruction* (pp. 94–97). Novato, CA: Arena Press.

*Generally accepted pronunciations of names, technical terms, and foreign words are provided. In some instances, alternative pronunciations may exist.

The Phrase It! button reminds students to read in phrases and gets them started by having a narrator model the reading of the first few sentences.

The Word Clue feature—two to three per article—offers strategies for using context clues to figure out the meaning of unknown words.

Introducing standard features of nonfiction, such as headings, teaches students how text is organized and provides them with aids to comprehension.

Naismith thought some more. What if you *couldn't* run with the ball? Such a rule would force a team to move the ball only by **passing**. Then, there would be no need for tackling. And the team without the ball would have a chance to **steal** the passes.

Now, all he needed was a goal. He knew that a soccer goal would not work. Kicking or throwing a ball full force indoors would cause **injuries**. Perhaps he could place the goal several feet above the floor. Players would have to toss the ball in a gentle **arc** to score.

So, Naismith nailed two peach baskets to the **balcony** rails at each end of the gym. He explained his rules to the 18 class members. And on that day, more than 100 years ago, the first basketball game began—with a soccer ball.

The players scored only one basket in that first game. But as Naismith watched his teams, a thrilling thought ran through his mind. The players were having fun!

From Sticks to Skates

James Naismith's love for sports began while he was growing up in Canada. As a boy, he liked fishing and canoeing.

Jim's parents died when he was about nine years old. So, he lived with his grandmother and then moved in with his uncle. His **inventiveness** first came to life one winter night while watching his friends skate on a river. Jim wished he could afford a pair of skates. But he couldn't. So, he came up with an idea instead.

He raced to his uncle's shop. There, he found two old steel files. He sharpened the edges. Then, he made **grooves** in two sticks of wood. Jim set the files into the wood and tied the sticks onto his boots. Soon, he was skating on the ice with his friends.

From Teenager to Teacher

Before Jim turned 15, he had to leave school. He had to earn money to help his family.

Sentences do not continue across pages, making it easy for students to track print.

Students can touch each photograph to hear an audio caption with fun and useful information.

Research shows…

Students learn the meaning of thousands of new words each year. Since not every vocabulary word can be taught directly, teaching students how to learn new words independently is critical to their vocabulary growth. Some strategies for learning new words include using context, using word parts, and using the dictionary or glossary.

• See Beck, I. L., McKeown, M. G., & Omanson, R. C. (1987). The effects and uses of diverse vocabulary instructional techniques. In M. G. McKeown & M. E. Curtis (Eds.), *The nature of vocabulary acquisition* (pp. 147–163). Hillsdale, NJ: Erlbaum.

The Break It Down feature helps students use word analysis skills (prefixes, suffixes, syllabication, compound words) to break down and decode words.

Research shows...

Struggling readers need strategies to read new and/or longer words. The more automatic word recognition becomes, the more the reader can focus on comprehension.

• See Stanovich, K. (2000). Matthew effects in reading: Some consequences of individual differences in the acquisition of literacy. In K. Stanovich, *Progress in understanding reading: Scientific foundations and new frontiers* (pp. 149–206). New York: Guilford Press.

After several years, he returned to finish high school. Then, he moved to Montreal to go to college. While studying, Jim joined in several sports. One game he enjoyed was lacrosse, which was invented by Native Americans.

After college, Naismith taught **physical education** at the Young Men's Christian Association (YMCA) Training School in Springfield, Massachusetts. It was there that he created the game of basketball.

A few years later, Naismith decided to study medicine. He used what he learned to help young athletes.

A New Ball and New Rules

As Naismith's students graduated and took jobs at YMCAs throughout the country, the game's popularity grew. Within two years, the sport had its own ball. Iron goals soon replaced the baskets.

Naismith kept busy answering questions about the game. He also helped to set its rules. At first, there were as many as nine players in action on a team. By 1895, five people were in play for each team. Since then, that number has remained the same.

The biggest changes in the game have come from players. One of the first moves they created was the **dribble**. When guarded too closely, a player would dribble, or bounce, the ball while running. This allowed the player to keep control of the ball. Then, he would toss the ball to another player who could quickly give it back.

The "Father of Basketball"

In 1898, Naismith took a new job at the University of Kansas. There he spent the rest of his days, teaching and coaching. In time, the game he had invented spread around the world.

In 1936, basketball became a part of the Olympic Games in Berlin, Germany. From then on, Naismith was known as the "Father of Basketball."

Today, boys and girls, and men and women throughout the world enjoy playing basketball. And they have James Naismith to thank.

Comprehension strategy tips, for skills such as summarizing, are offered via audio in dialogue format throughout the book.

Research shows...

Comprehension instruction greatly increases readers' understanding of text. Embedding comprehension strategies in the text allows students to see exactly how and when to use them, and also helps students to become aware of their thought processes. Such instruction builds the habits of good readers naturally.

• See Wood, K. D. (1986, Summer). The effect of interspersing questions in text: Evidence for "slicing the task." *Reading Research and Instruction, 25,* 295–307.

The Super Challenge consists of six comprehension and vocabulary questions—presented via audio in a gamelike format—that test students' understanding of each article.

Questions include a balance of literal, inferential, and critical thinking skills to reinforce the comprehension skills practiced in the lesson.

Audio hints give students information about WHY an answer is right or wrong and help lead students to the correct answer. Sound effects enhance students' enjoyment and provide motivation.

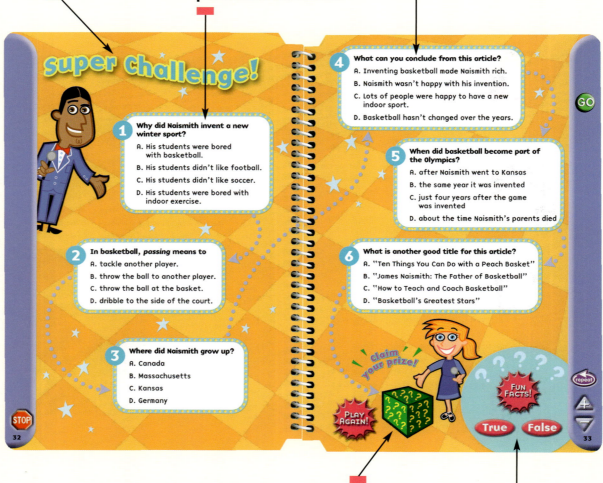

Students win a prize based on the total number of points they've earned in play. If a student scores zero, he or she is encouraged to go back and reread the selection.

In Fun Facts, four true/false questions extend readers' knowledge about the topic.

A fun, interactive game called Super Challenge Championships invites students to test their knowledge of new words and word analysis skills.

Research shows…
Word games help to foster "word consciousness" in students—an interest in words and a positive attitude toward learning new words.

- See Graves, M., Juel, C., & Graves, B. (1997). Vocabulary development. In M. Graves, C. Juel, and B. Graves, *Teaching reading in the 21st century*. Boston: Allyn and Bacon.
- Nagy, W. E., & Herman, P. S. (1987). Breadth and depth of vocabulary knowledge: Implications for acquisition and instruction. In M. G. McKeown & M. E. Curtis (Eds.), *The nature of vocabulary acquisition* (pp. 19–35). Hillsdale, NJ: Lawrence Erlbaum.

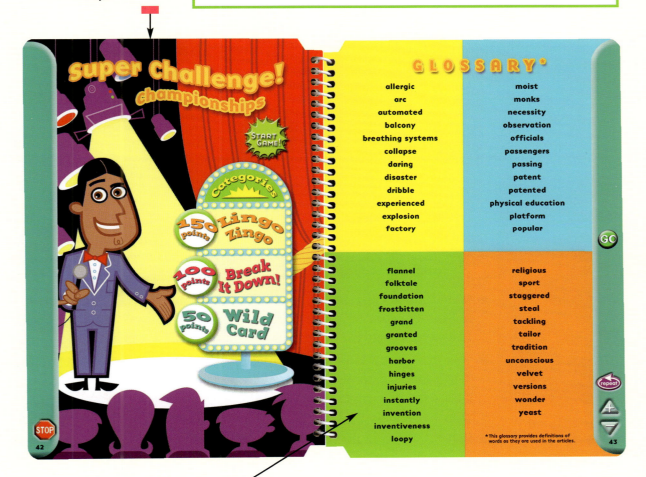

A glossary at the back of each book allows students to touch each word to hear its meaning.

You're ready to begin…
Now that you've "read it all," you're ready to begin. Spend some time getting to know the Quantum Pad™ platform. Read and enjoy the articles, and try out all the interactive features. See why *Read-It-All*™ *Books* will help your students make the leap to becoming confident, eager readers!

Amazing Inventions in this book

Articles	ATOS Readability	Word Analysis Skills	Comprehension Skills	Vocabulary
Crunch! The Pretzel Story	3.6	Suffix: -y	Sequence Compare and Contrast Context Clues	automated, folktale, instantly, loopy, moist, monks, popular, religious, tradition, yeast
Chester Greenwood's Ears	3.5	Prefix: in- Suffix/Inflectional Ending: -ed	Details Main Idea Context Clues	allergic, flannel, frostbitten, granted, hinges, invention, necessity, patent, sport, velvet
Wheels in His Head	3.5	Suffix: -tion	Draw Conclusions Fact and Opinion Context Clues	collapse, daring, experienced, foundation, grand, observation, officials, passengers, platform, wonder
The Way the Ball Bounced	3.7	Syllabication	Make Inferences Summarize Context Clues	arc, balcony, dribble, grooves, injuries, inventiveness, passing, physical education, steal, tackling
The Mask That Saved Lives	3.6	Compound Words (1 word)	Cause and Effect Predict Outcomes Context Clues	breathing systems, disaster, explosion, factory, harbor, patented, staggered, tailor, unconscious, versions

16

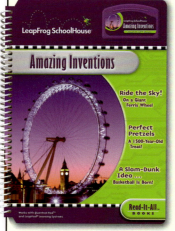

Articles adapted from Highlights® for Children

about this book

THEME: **Unusual inventions**

Cold ears? Bored students? For inventors, a problem is just an invention waiting to happen! The results may seem unusual, but inventors add fun and flavor to our lives, and sometimes save them! Each invention in this book has a story behind it.

- **"Crunch! The Pretzel Story"** reveals the secret history of this tasty snack. The article travels back in time to find the pretzel's origin in the monasteries of southern Europe, then moves forward to explore its use and form over the centuries.

- **"Chester Greenwood's Ears"** were the problem. They always got cold when Chester went outside to brave Maine's frosty winter weather. But when Chester combined wire, fur, and flannel to create an amazing accessory, his problem was solved, and the earmuff was born.

- In 1893, officials for the Chicago World's Fair were shocked when a young inventor first described his idea for a massive observation wheel. **"Wheels in His Head"** describes how George Ferris took an idea from his imagination and brought the Ferris wheel to life.

- When a young gym teacher needed a new indoor game to keep his students active during winter, he came up with basketball. **"The Way the Ball Bounced"** explains how one man's inspiration forever changed the world of sports.

- While it may have looked strange, there was nothing silly about Garrett Morgan's invention of the gas mask. His "Safety Hood" became **"The Mask That Saved Lives"** when he demonstrated its worth to firefighters in a daring tunnel rescue. Today, rescue workers and soldiers are forever grateful for Morgan's invention.

Whether tasty, entertaining, or essential, each of these inventions plays a part in our lives. Encourage students to find out the untold story behind each amazing invention.

Read-It-All™ Books

Create Interest in the Theme

Discuss the cover of the book and its title. Refer to the article summaries on page 16 of this manual to introduce and discuss two or three of the inventions in the book. Then, ask students,

Do you use any of these inventions or any others? How do they make your life easier?

Preview and Predict

Have students preview the book by looking at the titles in the Table of Contents and photographs throughout the book. Ask students to use a separate sheet of paper to write the name of each invention in the book. Have students predict the problems they think might have led to these inventions, then check their predictions as they read each article.

Have students use the **Articles I've Read** blackline master on page 29 of this manual to keep track of their reading.

Use the **How to Use *Read-It-All*™ Clues** blackline master on page 31 of this manual for an explanation of how to use the tips in the book. Then, copy and distribute the **Now I Know!** blackline master on page 32. Review instructions as necessary.

Integrate the Skills: Reading and Language Arts

Word Work: Syllabication

Explain that dividing longer words into syllables makes them easier to read. Point out that each syllable must have a vowel sound. Write the words *rabbit* and *napkin* on the board. Explain that if a word has the vowel-consonant-consonant-vowel (VCCV) pattern, we usually divide it between the consonants. Next, write the words *tiger* and *habit*. Explain that if a word has one consonant between two vowels (VCV pattern), we first divide it after the vowel and pronounce the vowel with its *long* sound. If that pronunciation is not right, then we divide the word after the consonant and pronounce the vowel with its *short* sound. Copy and distribute the **Word Work** blackline master on page 33. Review instructions as necessary.

 Remind English-language learners that vowel teams represent a single vowel sound in English, while in Spanish the vowels have two separate sounds (*ie* as in *pie* and *ti-EN-e*).

Enrichment: Once students can read two-syllable words, they are on their way to reading longer words. Have students work in pairs to find these three- and four-syllable words from the articles: *invention, observation, popular, legislature, allergic, factory, inventiveness, explosion*. Encourage students to syllabicate the first two syllables of each word, and then use what they know about suffixes to help figure out how to syllabicate the rest of the word.

Reading Strategy: Sequence

Explain to students that sequence is the order in which events happen. Draw this sequence chart on the board:

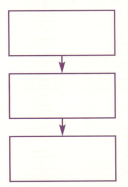

Remind students that they have read about how several inventions were created. Ask students to think about some of the things the inventors do during the process; for example, *they identify a problem, invent a solution, and show their invention to or test it on a group of people.* Write student responses on the board. Have students order the steps they have mentioned. Which one might come first? Next? Last? Then, copy and distribute the **Reading Tip** blackline master on page 34 of this manual. Review instructions as necessary.

 Using sequence words such as *first, next, before, later, afterward,* model a common activity, e.g., getting ready for school. Then, have English-language learners use sequence words to describe an activity of their choice.

Enrichment: Ask students to create a timeline that shows the sequence of important events in the life of one of the inventors mentioned in the articles.

Write About It!

Hello World

Ask students to imagine that each invention described in the book (*pretzel, gas mask, earmuffs, basketball, Ferris wheel*) is a brand-new invention. Then, invite them to make a poster to announce one of these inventions to the public. Have students brainstorm what information they will include in their posters. Tell them to ask themselves, *Who will buy the invention? Why will people want it?* Encourage students to write creative copy—using prose or poetry—and to use descriptive words, too. Remind students that a good poster needs a strong picture and just a few words. Have students first plan the poster on a small sheet of paper, encouraging them to use all the space, before drawing on a larger sheet. Hang posters on classroom walls.

Time Capsule

Explain to students that time capsules are containers that are filled with present-day objects. The capsules are then buried to help people in the future understand life in the past. Invite students to work in groups to choose five modern inventions that they would include in a time capsule for today. Point out that each invention should provide important insight into the way we live today for the people who uncover the capsule. Students should write a few sentences about each invention to include with the capsule. To help students get started, copy and distribute the **Write About It!** blackline master on page 35 of this manual.

You Are There!

Ask students to imagine they are news reporters, experiencing one of the inventions from the book for the very first time, e.g., they are taking the first ride on a Ferris wheel; they are in the crowd, watching the first game of basketball; they are on site at a tunnel disaster and see Morgan's Safety Hood for the first time. Have students write an on-the-scene report, describing the event and the invention. Remind students to include the 5Ws of good reporting—*who, what, where, when,* and *why*—in their articles. Encourage volunteers to read their articles to the class. Record student work in a "nightly news broadcast" show on audio or video.

Do a Project!

Invention Convention

Tell students that during the next month they will work in groups to create exhibits for an Invention Convention. Explain that a convention is a large gathering of people with common interests. Have each group select an invention as the subject of its exhibit—an invention that the group believes is "the most important ever."

To get started, copy and distribute the **Do a Project!** blackline master on page 36 of this manual. Review with students the process of creating an exhibit.

Brainstorm and Select Explain to students that at this stage, they should work together in a group to choose an invention that they believe has been critically important in history. The invention can date as far back as the wheel or it may be as recent as the MP3 player. Encourage each student to make suggestions; then have the group select one.

Research Explain to students that they should now gather information about the invention: its inventor or inventors, the era in which it was created, its changes and improvements over the years, and its benefits to the world.

Plan Using their research, students should begin planning what their exhibit will look like and what they wish to include. Invite students to consider multimedia possibilities, including photographs, audio, video, slideshows, or interactive computer programs. Groups should assign roles to each member to create visual aids, as well as written or recorded text.

Assemble and Examine Students should work together to complete and then review each aspect of their work. Encourage students to invite a few observers to preview their exhibit.

Display and Discuss Have groups take turns presenting their exhibits to classmates. Afterward, initiate a class discussion about what students learned from creating their own exhibits and from viewing the exhibits of others.

Connect to Content

Geography: The United States of Invention
Point out to students that inventions pop up in different places. Basketball, for example, comes from Massachusetts, and earmuffs come from Farmington, Maine. Then, copy and distribute the **Connect to Content** blackline master on page 37 of this manual. Have students locate on the map the "birthplace" of the eight American inventions listed. Also, have them add five of their own, including at least one invention from your home state!

Math: Survey of Inventions
Ask students to conduct a survey, asking friends and family members to choose the most important invention of their lifetimes. Students should interview at least 20 people from different age categories and record their findings in a tally table that lists the inventions and number of people who chose the invention. Then, have students plot their data on a horizontal bar graph—inventions on the y (vertical) axis and number of people who chose the invention on the x (horizontal) axis.

Science: What Makes It Work?
Have students research another invention they know very little about. Then, have them present their findings to the class, explaining the invention. Encourage presenters to give some main facts about the invention and include diagrams, models, video, or charts to help other students better understand how each invention functions.

The Arts: Gallery of the Future
Ask students to make predictions about inventions that might exist 100 years from now. Write responses on the board. Then, have students choose from the list and create a painting or illustration of one of the devices. Some students may wish to create a model of the future inventions. Create a "Gallery of the Future" in your classroom to display completed student work.

Know It All
For more activities to extend the learning, see the inside back cover of the student book.

Assessment Tips
- Maintain a checklist to keep track of which articles and activities each student completes by using the **Class/Student Record Sheet** blackline master on page 28 of this manual.
- Have students save samples of their writing in a portfolio or folder. Review the work with students from time to time. Ask them to discuss which piece of writing they are most proud of and why. Encourage them to explain what they learned while writing it.
- Suggest that students make a list of new words they learned. Encourage students to incorporate these new words into their speech and writing.
- Have students write a review of one of the articles they read by completing the **My Review** blackline master on page 30 of this manual.

BIBLIOGRAPHY

BOOKS
- ☆ *Brainstorm!: The Stories of Twenty American Kid Inventors*
  by Tom Tucker, Sunburst, 1998. **NONFICTION**
- ☆ *Almost Famous*
  by David Getz, Holt, 1993. **FICTION**
- ☆ *The Big Book of Cool Inventions : 77 Inventions, Experiments, and Mind-Bending Games*
  by Margaret and William Kenda, McGraw-Hill, 2000.
  SCIENCE PROJECTS
- *Inventing the Future: A Photobiography of Thomas Alva Edison*
  by Marfe Delano and David Sloane, National Geographic, 2002.
  BIOGRAPHY

☆ Read-Aloud book

WEB SITES
Wacky Patents
(www.delphion.com/gallery)
Inventors Museum
(www.kids.parentcafe.com)
Invention at Play
(www.inventionatplay.org)
Naismith Memorial Basketball Hall of Fame
(www.hoophall.com/history/history.htm)
Inventing Modern America: Games
(web.mit.edu/invent/www/ima/games.html)

Outdoor Adventures *in this book*

Articles	ATOS Readability	Word Analysis Skills	Comprehension Skills	Vocabulary
The Hummingbird Trail	3.1	Syllabication	Cause and Effect Draw Conclusions Context Clues	brilliant, hovered, inhabit, invisible, official, position, region, source, struggle, trek
Blind to Limitations	3.4	Compound Words (1 word)	Compare and Contrast Make Inferences Context Clues	adventurer, avalanche, challenge, experience, extraordinary, incredible, obstacles, sense, summit, supported
Lost in the Everglades	3.2	Ending: *-ous*	Sequence Predict Outcomes Context Clues	channel, dismal, drifted, maze, poisonous, prairie, prickle, slithered, swamp, wilderness
Journey to the Top of the World	3.5	Ending: *-ion*	Fact and Opinion Recall Details Context Clues	barrens, caribou, elders, fend, fierce, gust, lumbered, migration, pass, peaks
Up Close to Hubbard Glacier	3.8	Word Parts and Derivations	Main Idea Summarize Context Clues	face, fjord, glacier, iceberg, kayak, mass, retreat, rugged, rumble, tide

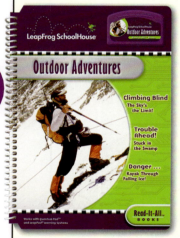

Articles adapted from Highlights® for Children

about this book

THEME: **Experiencing the great outdoors**

Whether it's climbing to the frozen top of North America, canoeing through the alligator-infested channels of the Everglades, or kayaking through icy waters to explore a glacier, the adventurers in this book have all experienced the great outdoors in extreme ways!

- When a hiker journeys along a 1,000-year-old trail in New Mexico to trace the steps of ancient travelers, she loses her way. But thanks to some tiny birds, she is led back to the path that early explorers called **"The Hummingbird Trail."**

- Eric Weinhenmayer is no ordinary explorer. Even though he lost his sight at age thirteen, Eric has explored jungles and hiked Peru's Inca Trail. So, it's no surprise that Eric would tackle North America's highest mountain. With this dangerous trek, Eric would prove that he's **"Blind to Limitations."**

- Two adventurous friends on a canoe trail become **"Lost in the Everglades."** As they paddle through a maze of channels, they come face to face with a huge alligator! Later, hungry and tired, they prepare to wait through the night—and hope for rescue.

- A husband-and-wife team takes a **"Journey to the Top of the World."** Their trip to the Arctic Ocean takes them across an icy, barren land with fierce winds. Along the way, they encounter grizzly bears, caribou, and "an endless world of white."

- A kayak-paddling adventurer braves the icy waters of a fjord to get right **"Up Close to Hubbard Glacier."** There, an ice chunk breaks away from the glacier, becoming an iceberg in the sea. As the glacier roars and rumbles, the adventurer watches as more icebergs form.

On icy lands or grassy waters, the adventurers in this book experience both challenges and triumphs. Encourage students to read all about their adventures.

Read-It-All™ Books

Create Interest in the Theme

Discuss the cover of the book and its title. Refer to the article summaries on page 20 of the manual to introduce and discuss two or three outdoor adventures described in this book. Then, ask students,

What outdoor adventures have you read about, seen on TV, or experienced yourself?

Preview and Predict

Have students preview the book by looking at both the titles in the Table of Contents and the photographs throughout the book. Ask students to write what they think each article will be about on a sheet of paper. Have them check their notes as they read to see if their predictions are correct.

Article	Predictions

Have students use the **Articles I've Read** blackline master on page 29 of this manual to keep track of their reading.

Use the **How to Use *Read-It-All*™ Clues** blackline master on page 31 of this manual for an explanation of how to use the tips in the book. Then copy and distribute the **Now I Know!** blackline master on page 32. Review instructions as necessary.

Integrate the Skills: Reading and Language Arts

Word Work: Compound Words

Explain that a compound word is made up of two smaller words. Tell students that they can sometimes figure out the meaning of a compound word from the meaning of its two smaller words, e.g., *classroom* is a "room for a class." Write the following on the board:

hummingbird   sleeping bag   one-way

Explain that there are three types of compounds: one-word (*hummingbird*); two-word (*sleeping bag*); and hyphenated (*one-way*). Make sure students can identify each example, and use the smaller words to figure out the meaning of each compound. Copy and distribute the **Word Work** blackline master on page 38 of this manual to give students practice defining compound words.

 Encourage English-language learners to identify, pronounce, and define school-related compound words, e.g., *backpack, fire drill*, etc.

Enrichment: Brainstorm with students a list of compound words. Then invite students to define each compound word using picture puzzles. Encourage students to illustrate each small word within the compound word. [Note: Some words won't lend themselves to meaningful picture puzzles, e.g., *straw + berry*; but such compound puzzles do make fun word games.]

watch   dog

Reading Strategy: Summarizing

Remind students that a summary is a short statement of important events or ideas in a story or article. Read aloud the following passage:

Tony and Sara paddled their kayak through the wild waters of Wisconsin's Wolf River. The waves slammed against their small boat, drenching them. As the kayak twisted and bobbed in the roaring white waters, Tony yelled, "What an adventure!"

Copy and distribute the **Reading Tip** blackline master on page 39. Using the five rules for writing a summary on the blackline master, work with students to write a summary of the passage, e.g., *Tony and Sara struggled to paddle their kayak through Wolf River.* Write students' responses on the board. Then, have students do the activity on the blackline master.

 Make sure English-language learners understand each sentence in the passage before they attempt to summarize.

Enrichment: Clip newspaper articles for pairs of students. Do not include the headlines. Have students take turns reading aloud each article and then writing a headline that summarizes it. Point out that a headline usually gives a summary of the article. Have students share their completed headlines with the class.

Write About It!

Wish You Were Here!

Remind students that postcards are often sent from someone on the road to people at home. A postcard often shares information about what its writer has seen or experienced in another place. Have students imagine that they are adventurers in one of the articles. Have them use 5" x 7" index cards to write a "postcard" to a friend, family member, or caregiver to share their experiences. Invite them to create an illustration on one side of the card and write their note on the other. Have students address the cards as if for mailing.

You Can't Live Without This!

Remind students that persuasive writing presents an opinion and tries to convince the reader to agree with it. Persuasion is often used in TV commercials and print advertisements. Invite students to imagine that they have an item from the book to sell, for example, a vehicle, such as a kayak or an airboat, or equipment, such as climbing or camping gear. Invite students to write a sales pitch for their item that includes its description, as well as facts and examples to support what makes it special. Ask students to also include suggestions for the kinds of adventures that can be had with the item. Invite students to read aloud their completed sales pitches in a strong tone of voice that would be likely to persuade their audience.

"My Outdoor Adventure" Scrapbook Page

Have students brainstorm a list of various outdoor adventures—from camping in their own backyards to riding in a helicopter. Then invite students to write a first-person narrative to describe one of these adventures. Ask students to describe in detail three exciting things that could happen on the adventure. Then have students include these in their narratives. Remind students that a narrative should pull readers into the story and keep them wondering what will happen next. Encourage students to draw their own illustrations or use photographs to create a scrapbook page so that they can share their experiences. Display the completed scrapbook pages in a collected edition in your classroom or on your school's Web site.

Do a Project!

Adventure Bound!

Tell students that over the next month they will work in groups to plan an outdoor adventure. They will prepare interactive presentations and travel brochures to share their plans. Copy and distribute the **Do a Project!** blackline master on page 40 of this manual. It offers an explanation of each stage of the project as well as a checklist for students to note their progress.

Choose a Destination With the class, visit *www.outwardbound.com* to consider destinations and adventures, e.g., dog sledding, rock climbing, whitewater rafting, etc. Then, for more ideas, have students meet in their groups to visit the Web sites included in the bibliography.

Research Explain to students that their research should include how they will arrive at their destinations, how long they will stay, where they will stay, what clothing and equipment will be required, the sport they will do, how much their adventure will cost, and who will accompany them. Have students include safety tips as well.

Write, Draw, and Edit Have students meet in their groups to assign different writers for each part of their presentation and to begin writing. Have each group assign an artist to create a travel brochure. Work with one group to model the process of peer editing. Then have group members work together to edit and revise their work.

Assemble Have students work together to assemble and finalize the interactive presentation. Remind the groups that their presentations might include videotape, slides, or photographs with recorded music. Or, if possible, they might use software to create graphics, sound effects, and film.

Present When giving their presentations, students should be reminded to speak clearly, to use hand and arm gestures to emphasize a point, and to look at their audience. After all the projects have been presented, lead a discussion on the importance of taking safety precautions during an adventure.

Connect to Content

Everglades Adventure
Tell students they are going to plan a trip to the Everglades. If possible, have students visit the Web site at *www.everglades.nationalpark.com* to learn more about different places of interest inside the park. Then, copy and distribute the **Connect to Content** blackline master on page 41 of this manual. Review the map with students, pointing out the map scale and how to use it.

Acting Adventurers
Adventurers have faced many challenges. Ask students to choose a famous adventurer to research. Have them use resources, such as biographies, videos, Web sites, etc. Then, invite students to role-play their adventurers, presenting first-person accounts of their adventures. Some students may wish to "come in costume." If possible, videotape or record the presentations to share with other classes.

"Animal Fact" Poster
Ask students to revisit the animals they encountered in the book and select one to research. Copy and distribute the **Connect to Content** blackline master on page 42 of this manual. Have students use resource materials, including books, encyclopedias, and Web sites to learn about the animal. Invite them to use the fact file on the blackline master to organize their information. Then, have them create a poster to share their findings. Encourage students to plan their posters on a small sheet of paper before they create the poster on a larger sheet. Display the completed posters.

Adventurous Environments
Remind students of the different habitats they encountered in the book—desert, Arctic, wetlands—and the specific location each adventurer explored. Invite students to recreate one of the locations, using dioramas, models, or murals. Have students research special facts about their chosen environments to find out the types of animals and plants that live there, or if the environment is endangered, for example. Then, display the projects.

Know It All
For more activities to extend the learning, see the inside back cover of the student book.

Assessment Tips
- Maintain a checklist to keep track of which articles and activities each student completes by using the **Class/Student Record Sheet** blackline master on page 28 of this manual.
- Observe students to identify the multiple intelligences that are their strengths: word, math, artistic, musical, movement, working with other people, working independently. Then, create activities that will provide a successful "fit."
- Have students write a review of one of the articles they read by completing the **My Review** blackline master on page 30 of this manual.

BIBLIOGRAPHY

BOOKS
Danger on the Mountain: Scaling the World's Highest Peaks
  by Andrew Donkin, DK, 2001. **NONFICTION**

Everglades
  by Jean Craighead George, HarperCollins, 1995. **FICTION**

Dreams of Hummingbirds: Poems from Nature
  by Mary Ann Coleman, Albert Whitman, 1993. **POETRY**

☆ *My Side of the Mountain*
  by Jean Craighead George, Penguin, 1988, 1959.
  CLASSIC FICTION

☆ *Shipwreck at the Bottom of the World: The Extraordinary True Story of Shackleton and the Endurance*
  by Jennifer Armstrong, Random House, 2000. **NONFICTION**

☆ **Read-Aloud book**

WEB SITES
El Malpais, New Mexico
  (http://elmalpais.areaparks.com)

Everglades National Park
  (www.everglades.national-park.com)

Expedition on Mt. McKinley
  (www.terragalleria.com/mountain/mountain-area.mckinley.html)

Gallery of Hubbard Glacier Photos
  (www.fs.fed.us/r10/tongass/forest_facts/photogallery/hubbard_photos.html)

Outward Bound
  (www.outwardbound.com)

Outdoor Adventures

Nature's Fury

in this book

Articles	ATOS Readability	Word Analysis Skills	Comprehension Skills	Vocabulary
The Snow Is Snowin', the Wind Is Blowin'	3.1	Syllabication	Main Idea Details Context Clues	drifts, experience, extremely, forecasting, fuel, hazardous, hurricane, shelter, stranded, telegraph
A Shock in the Dead of Night	3.6	Compound Words (1 word)	Sequence Predict Outcomes Context Clues	aftershock, device, energy, fireballs, phenomena, plates, prediction, recovery, remains, seismometer
Great Fires	3.5	Suffix: -ly	Cause and Effect Summarize Context Clues	conditions, contained, draft, droughts, embers, firebreaks, ignites, remote, tinder, walkie-talkie
"Wasn't That a Mighty Storm?"	3.8	Suffix: -less	Fact and Opinion Draw Conclusions Context Clues	civilized, debris, destruction, evacuate, founded, orphanage, position, relentless, rubble, seawall
Chasing the Tornado	3.3	Prefix: un-	Compare and Contrast Make Inferences Context Clues	column, funnel, hurls, mission, photojournalist, severe, tornado, twister, vortex, warnings

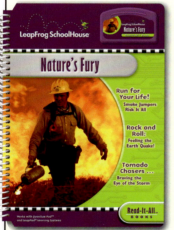

about this book

THEME: **Natural disasters**

Trembling earth, unbearable cold, intense heat—when Earth gets angry, its fury knows no limits. From fires to blizzards to earthquakes, each disaster in this book demonstrates the powerful force of nature's fury.

- **"The Snow Is Snowin', the Wind Is Blowin'"** explains just what happens when a blizzard strikes. The Schoolchildren's Blizzard of 1888 left children in the Great Plains stranded, while that same year the Great White Hurricane paralyzed the East Coast for days.

- In 1976, a million people in Tangshan, China, felt **"A Shock in the Dead of Night"** when a massive earthquake rocked the ground. Much of the city was destroyed. Now scientists in China are working to develop new earthquake prediction techniques.

- **"Great Fires"** are some of the most frightening experiences on Earth. The cities of London, Chicago, and San Francisco have all been the scene of massive blazes, but these fires can take place in the wilderness, too.

- The survivors of the Great Galveston Hurricane couldn't help but say, **"'Wasn't That a Mighty Storm?'"** This 1900 hurricane took residents by surprise, washing away nearly half the town. In no time, the people repaired the city and built a giant seawall to protect it. In 1915, when another hurricane struck, Galveston was prepared.

- While most people run away from disasters, photographers and storm spotters run toward them. **"Chasing the Tornado"** describes the work of two tornado chasers who document these funnel clouds to help keep people out of their perilous paths.

All the natural disasters in this book can be incredibly dangerous. Yet, there are ways to minimize the risk and stay out of harm's way. Encourage students to read all about these disasters.

Create Interest in the Theme

Discuss the cover of the book and its title. Refer to the article summaries on page 24 of this manual to introduce and discuss the natural disasters featured in this book. Ask students,

Are you ever scared by a storm? How can weather damage cities or buildings? Name a disaster you've heard about or experienced.

Preview and Predict

Have students preview the book by looking at the titles in the Table of Contents and at the photographs throughout the book. Ask students to use a separate sheet of paper to make predictions about the information each story will contain. Ask them to check and revise their predictions as they read.

Article	Predictions

Have students use the **Articles I've Read** blackline master on page 29 to keep track of their reading.

Refer to the **How to Use *Read-It-All*™ Clues** blackline master on page 31 of this manual to show students how to use the tips in the book. Then, copy and distribute the **Now I Know!** blackline master on page 32. Review instructions as necessary.

Integrate the Skills: Reading and Language Arts

Word Work: Content Area Vocabulary

Explain to students that when you read about a topic, such as a natural disaster, you can often learn lots of new words related to it.

Write *weather* in the center of a web on the chalkboard. List the words *hurricane, tornado,* and *blizzard* around it. Point out that each word represents a specific kind of weather. Have students suggest other words to add to the web. Next, copy and distribute the **Word Work** blackline master on page 43. Review instructions as necessary.

Discuss the natural disasters that occur in the native countries of English-language learners. Choose one disaster. Have students describe it to build vocabulary on this topic.

Enrichment: Invite students to create an illustrated dictionary of natural disaster terms from *Nature's Fury*. Have students choose four words to define. Tell students that each entry should include the correct spelling, syllable division, meaning, part of speech, synonyms, and antonyms. Then, ask students to create illustrations. Compile words into a booklet for classroom display.

Reading Strategy: Draw Conclusions

Explain to students that when you draw conclusions, you look carefully at several facts or details from a text to reach an understanding about something the writer doesn't directly state. Then, draw the following diagram on the board.

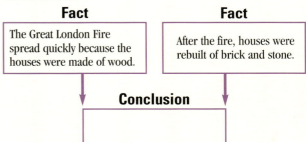

Point out that although the writer doesn't say so, you can conclude from the two facts that *London was safer from fires after it was rebuilt*. Ask students to draw other conclusions from the same two facts. Have a student do a think-aloud to explain his or her reasoning. Then, copy and distribute the **Reading Tip** blackline master on page 44 of this manual.

Explain to students what *to draw a conclusion* means and that it has nothing to do with drawing a picture. Point out other idioms that use *draw*, e.g., *draw a curtain* and *draw a card*.

Enrichment: Ask students to write the name of each kind of natural disaster described in the book on a piece of paper. Have students write one conclusion that can be drawn from their reading. Tell students to be sure that they can support their conclusions with facts from the articles. Have students list the facts they use beneath each conclusion they have drawn. Model this, using a think-aloud procedure.

Write About It!

Fear Factor
Ask students to think about which kind of natural disaster described in the book they find most frightening, and why. Then, have students write a paragraph explaining their choice. To help students get started, you can have them create a "fright web" to list all the reasons why their chosen disaster is so fearsome. Invite students to read their paragraphs to the class.

Howling Haiku
Explain to students that a *haiku* is an ancient form of Japanese poetry. In traditional haiku, the subjects are almost always from nature, frequently related to specific seasons of the year. Find several examples of traditional haiku in a book such as *Grass Sandals: The Travels of Basho* and read them aloud to students. Or, read the following haiku:

> Frost freezing fingers
> All the world is whisper white
> Snowflakes fill the sky

Review the haiku's three-line, 17-syllable form: 5-7-5. Then, have students write their own *Nature's Fury* haiku, inspired by the articles in the book. You may also distribute photographs of storms and other natural phenomena and have students base their poems upon these images. To help get students started, copy and distribute the **Write About It!** blackline master on page 45.

Dear Diary
Have students write a fictional diary entry based on the events from one of the articles in *Nature's Fury*. Students should brainstorm a character who is living through one of the disasters described in the book, and then write an entry that describes the character's experiences and feelings from the character's point of view. Encourage students to consider the setting of their chosen disaster, for example, China, 1976, or the American Midwest during the blizzard of 1888. To get them started, ask, How might a person in that particular time and place feel when disaster strikes? How might he or she respond?

Do a Project!

"Disaster" Documentary
Tell students that during the next month they will work together in groups to produce a television or radio newsmagazine-style documentary. The documentary can be recorded on audiotape or videotape, or can be broadcast/performed live before the class. The documentary's subject will be a real-life natural disaster. The show should be structured as a chronologically ordered narrative. Discuss the following steps:

Research and Choose Students should work in groups to choose a natural disaster as the subject of their documentary. All students should try to learn as much as they can about the subject. Suggest Internet and library resources to help students in their work. Then, have students use their research to choose three events from the disaster to present. Next, have them write down one or two paragraphs that present an overview of their documentary.

Create To help students get started, copy and distribute the **Do a Project!** blackline master on page 46 of this manual. Explain that each event will become a scene in the documentry. As students work together to create the scenes, remind them that each scene should answer the 5Ws: Who? What? Where? When? Why? Remind them, too, that each scene should have a great lead or introduction, facts and ideas to support it, and an ending.

Organize and Assign Roles Every group will need writers and researchers; some also might need actors to role-play newscasters who interview survivors and disaster experts. All groups will also need artists to build models or dioramas.

Rehearse or Record Have students meet with their groups to record their documentaries, for audio- or videotape, or rehearse them, if they are to be performed live.

Broadcast Have groups take turns "screening" their documentaries for their classmates. After students have watched the documentaries, have them discuss what they learned about natural disasters and the process of documenting them.

Connect to Content

Geography — Danger Zones
Explain to students that "Tornado Alley," "Earthquake Belts," and "Hurricane Highways" describe places where these kinds of disasters are most likely to occur. Copy and distribute the **Connect to Content** blackline master on page 47 of this manual. Focus students' attention on the map legend. Show students how different kinds of shading and graphics represent different kinds of disaster risks. Then, have students complete the activity.

Social Studies — Develop a Dialogue
Help students initiate an e-mail or letter correspondence with students at an equivalent grade level who live in Tornado Alley. (Choose a city or town in that region and call its Board of Education for contact information about an appropriate school and teacher for this activity.) Invite students to brainstorm tornado-related questions to ask their out-of-state peers; for example, "What do you do in a tornado drill?" and "What does the air feel like when tornadoes are near?" If you live in Tornado Alley, help students initiate a similar dialogue with peers who live in an area prone to earthquakes.

Math — Wild Weather?
Is the weather getting wilder, or have hurricanes and tornadoes always posed the same threats they do today? Have students use the Internet and books to research the number of tornadoes and hurricanes that have struck the United States over the last hundred years. Then, have students organize the data into a double-line graph to show whether wild weather is really on the rise.

The Arts — Scary Soundtrack
Natural disasters can produce powerfully strong sounds. Musically inclined students can compose a "scary soundtrack," a piece of music inspired by the sounds of a natural disaster. Others may create "scary sound effects," using everyday objects. Invite students to share their compositions, while classmates try to guess which disaster they have captured in sound.

Know It All

For more activities to extend the learning, see the inside back cover of the student book.

Assessment Tips

- Maintain a checklist to keep track of which articles and activities each student completes by using the **Class/Student Record Sheet** blackline master on page 28 of this manual.
- Meet with students periodically to observe them engaged in different stages of the reading process. Have students read sections of an article out loud to assess their fluency: Listen for whether they are mindful of punctuation; reading in phrases; etc.
- Have students write a review of one of the articles they read by completing the **My Review** blackline master on page 30.

BIBLIOGRAPHY

BOOKS

Grass Sandals: The Travels of Basho
 by Dawnine Spivak, Atheneum, 1997. POETRY

Eyewitness: Hurricane and Tornado
 by Jack Challoner, DK, 2000. NONFICTION

☆ *Hurricane Hunters and Tornado Chasers: Life in the Eye of the Storm*
 by Lois Sakany, Rosen, 2003. NONFICTION

Do Tornadoes Really Twist?: Questions and Answers About Tornadoes and Hurricanes
 by Melvin Berger, Scholastic, 2000. NONFICTION

☆ *In the Heart of the Quake*
 by David Levithan, Apple, 1998. FICTION

☆ Read-Aloud book

WEB SITES

Earthquakes
(www.thetech.org/exhibits/online/quakes)

The Galveston Hurricane
(www.1900storm.com)

Federal Emergency Management Agency (FEMA for Kids)
(www.fema.gov/kids)

National Severe Storms Laboratory Album (Tornado Photos)
(www.photolib.noaa.gov/nssl/tornado1.html)

Forest Firefighter Photo Journal
(www.sover.net/~kenandeb/fire/hotshot.html)

Date _____

CLASS/STUDENT RECORD SHEET

Name of Student	Articles Read	Activities Completed	Notes

Name _____ Date _____

ARTICLES I'VE READ

	Title of Article	Title of Book	Date Started/ Date Finished	Coolest Fact in This Article
1.				
2.				
3.				
4.				
5.				
6.				
7.				
8.				
9.				
10.				
11.				
12.				
13.				
14.				
15.				

Name _____ Date _____

My Review

Title of Article _____

Title of Book _____

This article is about _____
_____.

Two facts I learned from reading this article are

1. _____
_____

2. _____
_____

I thought the best part of this article was _____
_____
_____.

I would like to learn more about _____
_____
_____.

I would tell others to read this article because _____
_____
_____.

This article was (easy to read)   1   2   3   4   5   (hard to read).

Name _____ Date _____

How to Use *Read-It-All*™ Clues

Show students how to access the clues by following the procedure below. Explain that when students click on an icon, they will hear a professor and a curious student talking about a useful reading tip.

1. Point out the name of the icon.
2. Describe the skill the clue will teach.
3. Have students read the paragraph beside the icon.
4. Have students click on and listen to the tip. Then have students explain it.
5. Have students repeat the reading strategy on their own. Use the handout on the following page.

Icon	Skill	Purpose of Strategy
BREAK IT DOWN	Syllabication, Prefixes, Compounds, Derivations, Suffixes/Inflectional Endings	to use a variety of word analysis skills to decode words and figure out their meanings
WORD CLUE	Context Clues	to figure out the meaning of unfamiliar words using context clues
THE BIG IDEA	Main Idea	to find the main idea of a paragraph or article
FIND THE DETAILS	Details	to recall specific facts and details from an article
WHY DID IT HAPPEN?	Cause and Effect	to identify what happened (the effect) and why it happened (the cause)
WHAT'S NEXT?	Predict Outcomes	to predict what will happen next in an article
WHAT DO YOU THINK?	Draw Conclusions	to put together information in order to draw conclusions
SUM IT UP	Summarize	to choose the most important ideas in order to summarize a passage or an article
FACT OR OPINION?	Fact and Opinion	to distinguish facts from opinions
FIGURE IT OUT	Make Inferences	to "read between the lines" and infer what is not directly stated
SAME OR DIFFERENT?	Compare and Contrast	to compare and contrast people, places, events, and ideas
WHAT'S THE ORDER	Sequence	to identify the sequence of events in an article

Name _____ Date _____

Now I Know!

Title of Article _____

Title of Book _____

Word Clues: List three new words you learned from reading this article. Write the meaning beside each word. Then, describe the tip that helped you learn the new word.

   1. Word and Definition _____

   Tip _____

   2. Word and Definition _____

   Tip _____

   3. Word and Definition _____

   Tip _____

Break It Down: Explain how this tip helped you read a new and difficult word. Be sure to write the new word below.

_____

_____

Reading Tips: Put a check [✔] beside the reading tips that helped you the most.

____ The Big Idea   ____ Find the Details   ____ Why Did It Happen?

____ What's Next?   ____ What Do You Think?   ____ Sum It Up   ____ What's the Order?

____ Fact or Opinion?   ____ Figure It Out   ____ Same or Different?

Choose one of the tips you checked. Tell how it helped you better understand the article. _____

_____

Name _____   Date _____

Word Work

Find the Invention

Rules for dividing syllables:

1. If the word has the VCCV (vowel-consonant-consonant-vowel) pattern, divide it between the consonants.

2. If a word has one consonant between two vowels (VCV), first divide it after the vowel and pronounce the vowel with its *long* sound. If that pronunciation is not right, then divide the word after the consonant and pronounce the word with its *short* sound.

VCCV	VCV (long sound)	VCV (short sound)
Fer•ris	**pi•lot**	**hab•it**

Use the two rules to break each word below into syllables. Then, to check your work, write the syllables for each word in the correct row in the puzzle below. Read the word in the boxes to find the hidden invention!

travel _____   sky _____

protects _____   flannel _____ *flan•nel* _____

future _____   finish _____

systems _____   platform _____

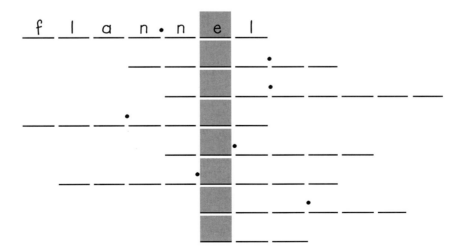

Read-It-All™ Books, Amazing Inventions • **33**

Name _____ Date _____

Reading Tip

What's the Order?

The order in which things happen is called the **sequence of events.** Understanding the sequence of events can help you identify and remember important events. For example, how does an inventor come up with a new invention? What might the inventor do first, second, third, and last?

Choose an invention from the book. Fill in the boxes to show, step-by-step, how that invention came to be.

Step 1

↓

Step 2

↓

Step 3

↓

Step 4

Name _____   Date _____

Write About It!   Time Capsule

A time capsule lets people in the future know about how we live today. Think of two inventions you would put in a time capsule. Include things you couldn't live without today. List them in the time capsules below, and tell why the inventions are important to you.

Invention # 1:
_____

Why I'm including it:
_____
_____
_____

Invention # 2:
_____

Why I'm including it:
_____
_____
_____

BRAIN TEASER
Which invention from the book would definitely NOT fit in a time capsule?
(Hint: It's way too big!)

Read-It-All™ Books, Amazing Inventions

Name _____ Date _____

Do a Project!

Invention Convention

To plan and create your exhibit for the *Invention Convention*, follow these steps:

Brainstorm and Select
- ❏ List possibilities for "The World's Most Important Invention." To help select one from the list, ask,
  - Why is this invention important?
  - How has it changed lives?
  - What would life be like without it?

Research Your Invention
- ❏ Gather information about the invention from at least three sources: books, encyclopedias, magazines, newspapers, the Internet.
  - Who invented it and why?
  - When and where was it invented?
  - How has it been used? How has it changed over the years?

Plan Your Exhibit
- ❏ Consider using at least three or four of the following:
  - written reports
  - video
  - photos
  - slide shows
  - computer animation
  - charts and graphs
  - audio
  - models
  - drawings
  - timelines
- ❏ Assign tasks to each group member.

- ❏ Review each part of your exhibit.
  - Is it useful?
  - Does it add interest and excitement?
  - Does it help convince others that your choice is the "most important invention ever"?

Assemble and Examine Your Exhibit
- ❏ Put together your exhibit.
- ❏ Make any needed improvements.
- ❏ Get comments from outside observers.
- ❏ Make more improvements, if necessary.

Display and Discuss Your Exhibit
- ❏ Present your exhibit.
- ❏ Ask your classmates what they learned from this exhibit.

Name _____   Date _____

Connect to Content

The United States of Invention

Many cities in the U.S.A. like to call themselves the "birthplace" of some modern invention. We know that the airplane was invented in Kitty Hawk, North Carolina, for example. But where was the banana split born? Where was the gas station invented?

▶ Find the state on the map that claims to be the birthplace of each invention. Label the map with the numbers of the inventions on the list.

Invention	Where it was invented
1. Airplane	Kitty Hawk, North Carolina
2. Blue Jeans	San Francisco, California
3. Gas Station	Seattle, Washington
4. Ice Cream Cone	St. Louis, Missouri
5. Softball	Chicago, Illinois
6. ATM Machine	Dallas, Texas
7. Banana Split	Latrobe, Pennsylvania
8. Buffalo Wings	Buffalo, New York

▶ Research the birthplaces of five more American inventions. Add them to the map above.

Name _____ Date _____

Word Work

Compound Words

Compound words are made up of two smaller words. When you know the meanings of the smaller words, you can often figure out the meaning of a compound word.

Compound Word	Word 1	Word 2	Meaning
snowshoes	snow	shoes	shoes made for snow

There are three kinds of compound words. The chart below lists examples of each one. Use the two smaller words to figure out the meaning of each compound word. Then, write each meaning in the chart.

One-Word Compound	Meaning	Two-Word Compound	Meaning	Hyphenated Compound	Meaning
waterproof		ski poles		ice-skate	
outdoor		day school		drip-dry	
airboat		high tide		baby-sit	
wildflowers		scuba diving		forty-five	

38 • Read-It-All™ Books, Outdoor Adventures

Name _____ Date _____

Reading Tip

Sum It Up!

> When you write a **summary**, you choose only the most important ideas from what you have read.

Choose one of the articles in *Outdoor Adventures*. Then, use the following five rules to help you write your summary of the article:

☆ Find the big idea in the article. Look for headings and topic sentences.

☆ If you can't find a topic sentence in each section, make one up.

☆ Include only important information. Leave out the details.

☆ Write important information only one time. Do not repeat yourself.

☆ Use one word to stand for a list of ideas, actions, or people. For example, use the word "animals" if the article mentions leopards, zebras, and lions.

My Summary

_____
_____
_____
_____
_____
_____

Name _____ Date _____

Do a Project!

Adventure Bound!

Follow these steps to put together an interactive presentation about an outdoor adventure. Check each box as you complete the step.

Choose a Destination
- ❏ Meet in your groups to discuss a destination.
- ❏ Visit Web sites, and look through books and magazines for ideas.
- ❏ Choose a destination.

Research
- ❏ Gather information about your adventure. Use books, magazines, and the Internet.
  - Figure out how you'll arrive at your destination and how long you'll stay.
  - Find out what kinds of clothing and equipment you'll need.
  - Learn about what extreme sport you'll do and how much the adventure will cost.
  - Find out about your guide.

Write, Draw, and Edit
- ❏ Meet with your group to decide what will be in your presentation.
  - Decide who will write each part of the presentation.
  - Decide who will design a travel brochure.
- ❏ Write a draft for your assignment.
- ❏ Work with a partner to edit and revise your work.

Assemble
- ❏ Work with your group to put the interactive presentation together.
- ❏ Input your text.
- ❏ Create your own art or use clip art.
- ❏ Include Web sites about the adventure.
- ❏ Take a picture of your group with a digital camera, and add it to the presentation.
- ❏ Optional: prepare your videotape, slides, or photographs, and choose recorded music.

Present
- ❏ Share your work with the rest of the class.
- ❏ List the main ideas on a note card to help you remember them.
- ❏ Speak clearly.
- ❏ Look directly at your audience.

Name _____ Date _____

Connect to Content

Everglades Adventure

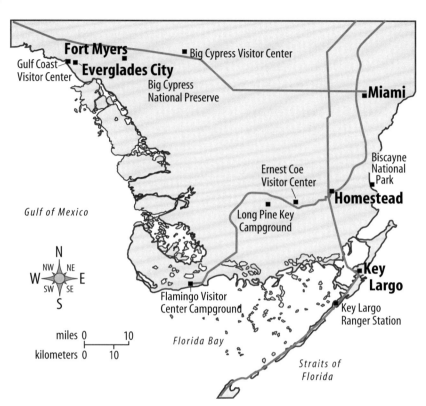

You're going on a trip to the Everglades! Use this map to plan your trip. Choose three places of interest. Plan a route that gets you from one place to the next in the fewest number of miles or kilometers.

▶ List the name of the city in Florida that is your starting point. Then, list all your points of destination and the distance from one place to the next.

Point of Destination	Distance
Starting point:	0 miles (kilometers) so far
First stop:	It's _____ miles (km) from my starting point.
Second stop:	It's _____ miles (km) from my 1st stop.
Third stop:	It's _____ miles (km) from my 2nd stop.

▶ How many miles (kilometers) will you cover? Add up the miles (kilometers) from your starting point to the places you'll visit. Use the back of this page to do the addition.

▶ Compare your plan with a partner's.

Name _____ Date _____

Connect to Content

Animal Fact File

Helpful Hints
A good poster needs a strong picture and just a few words. Remember: Plan your poster on a small sheet of paper. Use all the space. Put your title in big letters.

Choose one of the animals you read about in *Outdoor Adventures*. Research the animal to prepare a poster about it. Use the **Animal Fact File** below to help you organize your information. Place facts in each category as you do your research.

What It Looks Like

Where It Lives

What It Eats

What Its Enemies Are

Other Fun Facts

42 • Read-It-All™ Books, *Outdoor Adventures*

Name _____   Date _____

Word Work

Disaster Words

When you read about a nonfiction topic, you can learn lots of new words related to the subject. **Word webs** can help build your vocabulary by putting those words into categories.

▶ Now that you've read about nature's fury, you've learned some new words related to different types of disasters. Find four new words that describe fires and find four words that describe the storms of 1888. Write them on the lines provided.

▶ Now, use the back of this paper to write a radio announcement, warning listeners about a huge fire or blizzard that is headed straight for your town. Try to convince your listeners to act quickly to stay safe when disaster strikes!

Name _____ Date _____

Reading Tip

What Do You Think?

When you **draw conclusions** about a topic, you use facts in the text as clues to figure out something the writer doesn't state directly.

▶ What conclusion can you draw about natural disasters from the following facts?

FACT
Galveston built a huge seawall after the city was hit by a hurricane.

FACT
Chicago made new laws about fire safety after it was struck by a great fire.

CONCLUSION

▶ Use facts from two different articles in *Nature's Fury* to reach another conclusion about natural disasters. List your facts and conclusion below.

FACT

FACT

CONCLUSION

44 • Read-It-All™ Books, Nature's Fury

Name _____ Date _____

Write About It!

Howling Haiku

A **haiku** is a traditional Japanese poem that focuses on an image from nature. Every haiku has three lines, the first with 5 syllables, the second with 7, and the third with 5 syllables.

Haiku, Part 1
Ground be•neath your feet *(5)*
Trem•bles, shifts, slides to•geth•er *(7)*
Shock waves are ris•ing! *(5)*

Haiku, Part 2
Soon, a•bove the street *(5)*
Ev•ery•thing cracks and shat•ters *(7)*
As Earth o•pens wide. *(5)*

▶ What natural disaster does this haiku describe? _____

▶ Now, use the directions below to write your own haiku.

1. Choose a subject related to one of the natural events you read about in *Nature's Fury*. List words, phrases, and images that come to mind when you think about the subject.

   _____

   _____

   _____

2. Now use these words, phrases, and images to write your haiku. Make sure you have the right number of syllables in each line.

   1st line (5 syllables) _____

   2nd line (7 syllables) _____

   3rd line (5 syllables) _____

BRAIN TEASER
Only one kind of disaster in *Nature's Fury* can be caused by humans. Name it!

(Hint: Look in your book!)

Name _____ Date _____

Do a Project!

Disaster Documentary

Use the chart below to organize the three scenes of your documentary. Use the **Video** column of the chart to describe each scene of the disaster. Be sure to include the characters that will be in the scene, what they will look like, and what they will do. Then, use the **Audio** column to describe the dialogue, the music, and the sound effects you will use in each scene. An example has been done for you.

Video (What the audience will see)	Audio (What the audience will hear)
Example of snowstorm scene: Kids wearing coats holding on to rope. Wind blowing. Snow falling. Parents coming to rescue children.	*Example of snowstorm scene:* Wind howling. Grownups yelling, "Hang on!" Kids shouting, "Mom, Dad. Here I am!"
Scene 1	Scene 1
Scene 2	Scene 2
Scene 3	Scene 3

Name _____ Date _____

Connect to Content **Danger Zones**

Different kinds of disasters are likely to occur in different places. This map shows which states are most at risk for earthquakes, tornadoes, and hurricanes. Study the map. Then, on the back of this paper, answer the questions below.

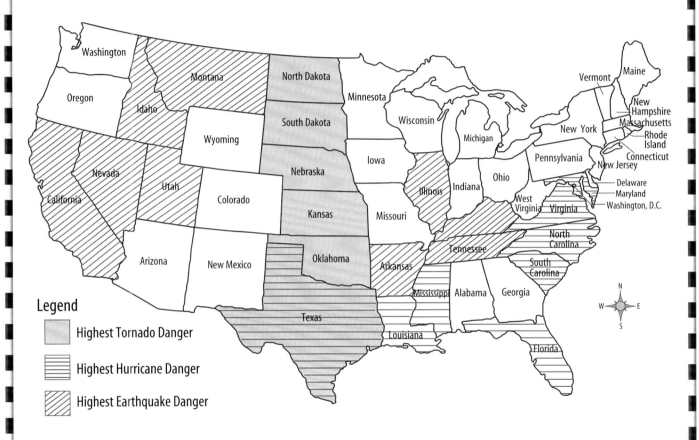

1. Name three states where earthquake risk is high.
2. Name three states where hurricane risk is high.
3. Name three states where tornado risk is high.
4. Name three states without high disaster risks.
5. Which state is at high risk for tornadoes and hurricanes?
6. Is your state at high risk for a disaster? If so, what kind?

Dear _____ ,

This year, students in my class will be using the *Read-It-All™ Books* program. The books include magazine-style articles on motivating topics. The books are designed to become interactive when placed on the Quantum Pad™ platform. By touching the words and symbols, your child can listen and learn new vocabulary and reading skills.

This week, it is your child's turn to take home the book *Amazing Inventions*. This book features articles about popular inventions and the stories behind their creation.

- "Crunch! The Pretzel Story" explores the long and interesting history of this popular snack.
- "Chester Greenwood's Ears" describes how one person's effort to warm his cold ears led to the invention of earmuffs.
- "Wheels in His Head" reveals the story behind the invention of the Ferris wheel, which people rode for the first time at the 1893 Chicago World's Fair.
- "The Way the Ball Bounced" describes how a gym teacher's effort to perk up his bored students led to the invention of basketball.
- "The Mask That Saved Lives" explores how Garrett Morgan convinced firefighters that his Safety Hood, which became the gas mask, could save lives.

Please read one article together each day. Explore the special features in the book, such as the reading tips, boldfaced words, "Super Challenges," and "Fun Facts." Share any information you may have about these inventions.

Have fun exploring inventions around your home. Choose an everyday item, such as a light bulb, the refrigerator, or the TV set. Then together, visit your local library or browse the Internet to learn the history behind the item. Who invented it and how?

Please be sure your child returns this book to class on

_____ .

Thank you, and happy reading!

Sincerely,

Estimado/a _____,

Este año, los alumnos en mi clase estarán usando el programa de *Read-It-All™ Books*. Los libros incluyen artículos en formato de revista sobre temas motivadores. Los libros han sido diseñados para volverse interactivos al colocarse sobre la plataforma Quantum Pad™. Al tocar las palabras y los símbolos, su hijo/a podrá escuchar y aprender vocabulario nuevo y nuevas destrezas de lectura.

Esta semana, le corresponde a su hijo/a llevar a casa el libro *Amazing Inventions*. Este libro presenta artículos acerca de invenciones insólitas y los antecedentes de su creación.

- "¡Crac! La historia de las rosquillas pretzel" explora la larga e interesante historia de esta golosina favorita.
- "Las orejas de Chester Greenwood" describe como los esfuerzos deuna persona para calentar sus orejas heladas lo llevaron a la invención de las orejeras.
- "Ruedas en la cabeza" revela la historia de la invención de la rueda de la fortuna, que hizo su estreno en la Feria Mundial de Chicago en 1893.
- "Cómo botó la bola" describe como los esfuerzos de un maestro de gimnasia por animar a sus alumnos aburridos lo llevaron a la invención del juego de baloncesto.
- "La máscara que salvó vidas" explica como Garrett Morgan convenció a los bomberos que su "Capucha de seguridad", que después se transformó en una mascarilla protectora de gas, podría salvar vidas.

Favor de leer un artículo juntos cada día. Exploren las secciones especiales del libro, como las claves de lectura, las palabras en negrilla, los "Super-Retos" y los "Datos divertidos". Cuéntele a su hijo/a otros datos o anécdotas que sepa sobre estas invenciones.

Diviértanse explorando invenciones en su casa. Escojan un artículo cotidiano, como una bombilla de luz, el refrigerador o el televisor. Luego, visiten juntos su biblioteca local, o rastreen el Internet para aprender la historia de ese artículo. ¿Quién lo inventó, y cómo?

Favor de asegurar que su hijo/a devuelva este libro a la clase el día

_____ .

Gracias, ¡y diviértanse con la lectura!

                                                            Atentamente,

Dear _____,

This year, students in my class will be using the *Read-It-All™ Books* program. The books include magazine-style articles on motivating topics. The books are designed to become interactive when placed on the Quantum Pad™ platform. By touching the words and symbols, your child can listen and learn new vocabulary and reading skills.

This week, it is your child's turn to take home the book *Outdoor Adventures*. This book features articles about exciting adventures and extreme sports in the great outdoors:

- "The Hummingbird Trail" tells of a hiker who traces the steps of ancient travelers along a route in New Mexico.

- "Blind to Limitations" follows Erik Weihenmayer, who lost his sight at the age of thirteen, as he treks to the top of North America's highest mountain.

- "Lost in the Everglades" reveals how two canoe-paddling pals found their way out of the alligator-infested channels of the Florida Everglades.

- "Journey to the Top of the World" explores a husband-and-wife team's hike across an "endless world of white" as they travel to the Arctic Ocean.

- "Up Close to Hubbard Glacier" tells of an adventurer who willingly paddles his kayak up close to a glacier to watch huge chunks of ice separate from it and form icebergs in the sea.

Please read one article together each night. Explore the special features and games throughout the book, such as the reading tips, boldfaced words, "Super Challenges," and "Fun Facts." Share any information you may have about other outdoor adventures.

Experience an outdoor adventure with your child. Take a trek along a nature trail, or go fishing, skiing, or sailing. Build a snowman, enjoy a bike ride, or watch the sun set. Ask your child to share his or her reactions to the things you encounter in nature on your outdoor adventure.

Please be sure your child returns this book to class on

_____.

Thank you, and happy reading!

                Sincerely,

Estimado/a _____,

Este año, los alumnos en mi clase estarán usando el programa de *Read-It-All™ Books*. Los libros incluyen artículos en formato de revista sobre temas motivadores. Los libros han sido diseñados para volverse interactivos al colocarse sobre la plataforma Quantum-Pad™. Al tocar las palabras y los símbolos, su hijo/a podrá escuchar y aprender vocabulario nuevo y nuevas destrezas de lectura.

Esta semana, le corresponde a su hijo/a llevar a casa el libro *Outdoor Adventures*. Este libro presenta artículos sobre aventuras emocionantes y los deportes extremos:

- "El sendero del colibrí" cuenta de una excursionista que sigue la ruta trazada por viajeros antiguos en Nuevo México.
- "Ciego a las limitaciones" acompaña a Erik Weihenmayer, quien perdió la vista a los trece años, al escalar la cima de la montaña más alta de norteamérica.
- "Perdido en el pantano Everglades" muestra cómo dos amigos en canoa hallaron la salida entre canales llenos de caimanes en el pantano Everglades de Florida.
- "Viaje a la cima del mundo" explora la caminata por un "infinito mundo blanco" realizada por un equipo formado por un matrimonio al viajar por el Mar Ártico.
- "El glaciar Hubbard de cerca" cuenta de un aventurero que acerca su piragua a un glaciar para observar la separación de enormes trozos de hielo que se caen al mar, formando témpanos, o icebergs.

Favor de leer un artículo juntos cada noche. Exploren las secciones especiales del libro, como las claves de lectura, las palabras en negrilla, los "Super-Retos" y los "Datos divertidos". Comparta cualquier información que tiene sobre otras aventuras al aire libre.

Realice una aventura al aire libre con su hijo/a. Caminen por un sendero en el monte, vayan de pesca, a esquiar o a pasear en barco de vela. Hagan un muñeco de nieve, paseen en bicicleta u observen la puesta del sol. Pídale a su hijo/a que comparta sus reacciones a las cosas que encuentran en la naturaleza o en su aventura al aire libre.

Favor de asegurar que su hijo/a devuelva este libro a la clase el día
_____.

Gracias, ¡y diviértanse con la lectura!

Atentamente,

Dear _____ ,

This year, students in my class are using the *Read-It-All™ Books* program. The books include magazine-style articles on motivating topics. The books are designed to become interactive when placed on the Quantum Pad™ platform. By touching the words and symbols, your child can listen and learn new vocabulary and reading skills.

This week, it is your child's turn to take home the book *Nature's Fury*. This book features five articles about different kinds of natural disasters.

- "The Snow Is Snowin', the Wind Is Blowin'" explains how two severe blizzards in 1888 stopped the United States in its tracks.
- "A Shock in the Dead of Night" describes a huge earthquake that rocked China and explores techniques scientists have used to predict earthquakes.
- "Great Fires" describes how these massive blazes affect both cities and wildlife.
- "Wasn't That a Mighty Storm?" explores the Great Hurricane of 1900 that took the city of Galveston, Texas, by surprise.
- "Chasing the Tornado" describes the dangerous work of tornado chasers, fearless professionals who run toward, rather than away from, tornadoes.

Please read one article together each day. Explore the special features in the book, such as the reading tips, boldfaced words, "Super Challenges," and "Fun Facts." Share any information you may have about the disasters described in the book.

Choose a weather-related or disaster-preparedness activity to do with your child. Track a storm together on television or over the Internet for several days. Work together on creating a disaster plan so that your family knows where to go in case of an emergency. Or, prepare a first-aid kit complete with bandages and antibiotic ointment.

Please be sure your child returns this book to class on

_____ .

Thank you, and happy reading!

                                                  Sincerely,

Estimado/a _____,

Este año, los alumnos en mi clase estarán usando el programa de *Read-It-All™ Books*. Los libros incluyen artículos en formato de revista sobre temas motivadores. Los libros han sido diseñados para volverse interactivos al colocarse sobre la plataforma Quantum Pad™. Al tocar las palabras y los símbolos, su hijo/a podrá escuchar y aprender vocabulario nuevo y nuevas destrezas de lectura.

Esta semana, le corresponde a su hijo/a llevar a casa el libro *Nature's Fury*. Este libro presenta cinco artículos sobre diferentes tipos de cataclismos naturales.

- "La nieve nevando, el viento soplando" explica como dos tremendas tormentas de nieve paralizaron el país en el año 1888.
- "Una sacudida en plena noche" describe un enorme terremoto que sacudió China y explora las técnicas utilizadas por los científicos para predecir los terremotos.
- "Incendios enormes" describe como estas conflagraciones afectan tanto las ciudades como los animales silvestres.
- "¿No fue una tremenda tormenta?" explora el "Gran huracán" de 1900 que sorprendió la ciudad de Galveston, Tejas.
- "Persiguiendo ciclones" describe el trabajo peligroso de los que persiguen los ciclones, profesionales valientes que buscan los ciclones en vez de huir de ellos.

Favor de leer un artículo juntos cada día. Exploren las secciones especiales del libro, como las claves de lectura, las palabras en negrilla, los "Super-Retos" y los "Datos divertidos". Comparta cualquier información que tiene sobre cualquiera de los cataclismos descritos en el libro.

Escoja una actividad para realizar con su hijo/a relacionada al tiempo o a las preparaciones para emergencias relacionadas a cataclismos. Sigan juntos durante varios días el progreso de una tormenta por televisión o Internet; establezcan un plan con un punto de reunión para su familia en caso de una emergencia; o prepare un equipo de primeros auxilios con vendas, analgésicos y pomada antibiótica.

Favor de asegurar que su hijo/a devuelva este libro a la clase el día

_____ .

Gracias, ¡y diviértanse con la lectura!

Atentamente,

Answer Key

Super Challenge!

The answers to the "Super Challenge!" questions are listed below. The skill each question addresses is indicated next to the answer.

Amazing Inventions

Crunch! The Pretzel Story (pages 8–9*)
1. A (vocabulary)
2. C (compare and contrast)
3. D (sequence)
4. B (draw conclusions)
5. B (vocabulary)
6. D (summarize)

Chester Greenwood's Ears (pages 16–17)
1. C (cause and effect)
2. D (details)
3. B (vocabulary)
4. C (vocabulary)
5. A (main idea)
6. D (draw conclusions)

Wheels in His Head: The Story of the Ferris Wheel (pages 24–25)
1. B (fact and opinion)
2. D (details)
3. A (vocabulary)
4. C (vocabulary)
5. B (draw conclusions)
6. D (sequence)

The Way the Ball Bounced (pages 32–33)
1. D (cause and effect)
2. B (vocabulary)
3. A (details)
4. C (make inferences)
5. A (sequence)
6. B (summarize)

The Mask That Saved Lives (pages 40–41)
1. D (vocabulary)
2. D (fact and opinion)
3. C (compare and contrast)
4. A (cause and effect)
5. B (vocabulary)
6. C (predict outcomes)

Outdoor Adventures

The Hummingbird Trail (pages 8–9)
1. C (vocabulary)
2. B (cause and effect)
3. A (vocabulary)
4. A (sequence)
5. B (draw conclusions)
6. D (main idea)

Blind to Limitations (pages 16–17)
1. D (cause and effect)
2. A (fact and opinion)
3. B (compare and contrast)
4. A (sequence)
5. C (vocabulary)
6. B (make inferences)

Lost in the Everglades (pages 24–25)
1. B (cause and effect)
2. A (sequence)
3. C (vocabulary)
4. D (details)
5. B (predict outcomes)
6. D (draw conclusions)

Journey to the Top of the World (pages 32–33)
1. C (details)
2. A (vocabulary)
3. C (cause and effect)
4. A (make inferences)
5. D (fact and opinion)
6. B (main idea)

Up Close to Hubbard Glacier (pages 40–41)
1. C (vocabulary)
2. B (details)
3. D (make inferences)
4. A (sequence)
5. D (summarize)
6. B (main idea)

Nature's Fury

The Snow Is Snowin', the Wind Is Blowin' (pages 8–9)
1. D (vocabulary)
2. A (compare and contrast)
3. D (details)
4. A (vocabulary)
5. B (draw conclusions)
6. A (main idea)

A Shock in the Dead of Night (pages 16–17)
1. A (fact and opinion)
2. D (details)
3. B (vocabulary)
4. D (cause and effect)
5. A (sequence)
6. D (predict outcomes)

Great Fires (pages 24–25)
1. B (compare and contrast)
2. C (vocabulary)
3. A (cause and effect)
4. C (details)
5. C (fact and opinion)
6. C (summarize)

"Wasn't That a Mighty Storm?" (pages 32–33)
1. C (vocabulary)
2. B (draw conclusions)
3. A (details)
4. D (sequence)
5. A (fact and opinion)
6. B (main idea)

Chasing the Tornado (pages 40–41)
1. D (sequence)
2. B (make inferences)
3. D (vocabulary)
4. A (summarize)
5. D (compare and contrast)
6. C (details)

* These numbers refer to pages in the interactive books.